A→Z OF BEING A GIRL OF GOD
DAWNIE REYNOLDS-DEAVILLE

Copyright © Dawn Reynolds-Deaville 2003.
ISBN 1 85999 764 3
Reprinted 2003, 2004
SUbtle products are youth publications of Scripture Union, 207-209
Queensway, Bletchley, MK2 2EB, England.
Email: info@scriptureunion.org.uk
Website: www.scriptureunion.org.uk

Scripture Union Australia
Locked Bag 2, Central Coast Business Centre, NSW 2252
Website: www.su.org.au

Scripture Union USA
P.O. Box 987, Valley Forge, PA 19482
www.scriptureunion.org

The right of Dawn Reynolds-Deaville to be identified as author of this
work has been asserted by her in accordance with the Copyright,
Designs and Patents Act 1988.
Scripture taken from THE MESSAGE. Copyright © 1993,1994,1995,1996,
2000, 2001, 2002. Used by permission of NavPress Publishing Group
Scripture quotations taken from the HOLY BIBLE NEW INTERNATIONAL VER-
SION. © 1973, 1978, 1984 by International Bible Society. Anglicisation
copyright © 1979, 1984, 1989. Used with permission of Hodder &
Stoughton Ltd.
British Library Cataloguing-in-Publication Data. A catalogue record for
this book is available from the British Library.

Cover design by Martin Lore
Internal design by Martin Lore
Printed and bound in Great Britain by Creative Print and Design
(Wales) Ebbw Vale

Scripture Union is an international Christian charity working
with churches in more than 130 countries providing resources to bring
the good news about Jesus Christ to children, young people and fami-
lies - and to encourage them to develop spiritually through the Bible
and prayer.
As well as our network of volunteers, staff and associates who run
holidays, church-based events and school Christian groups, we produce a
wide range of publications and support those who use our resources
through training programmes.

A→Z OF BEING A GIRL OF GOD

Contents

Acknowledgements

Phat luv & thanx to Mista Dee (Mark my fit bloke-hubby!), 4 lovin me & keepin me goin wiv ya cheekiness - u rock my world x. Me old dudes (mum & dad!) 4 bein there - I wouldn't have made it without u! Sara & Mark (the semolina pieheads!), wot can I say? Big love comin at ya, u & that table changed my life! Big ta's go out 2 my funky sista - Ems 'babydoll' Owen - u r the U in unique! Ta 4 all ya support. 2 my BIG SIS Elaine Storkey & BIG BRUV Andy Hawthorne. Ta 4 bein there in the gud times & bad times - u r mint! 2 past mateys who r still as cool as ever - Mads, Rach & Alex - skatin has never been so gud! U make me smile! Debs - the photocopying on the 'eve tour' started this - so we'd better finish it! - ta 4 bein u & inspiring me 2 become a carrier bag! U r the bomb! 2 all me mates at 'the Bethel', the Girlcrew, The Message & Norf Staffs YFC - ta 4 all ya support & love - love ya work man! 2 my bestest friend & saviour - the boss of the cross - Jesus Christ - u da man! So chuffed u love me - ta from the bottom of my trainers - no one can do it like u can! Last but no way least, I dedicate this book 2 my ickle sis 'Boo' - u know who u are - 2 who I owe my best coat! - luv ya longtime girl, X

hey u girls out there...

this is dawnie comin at ya with some advice on how 2 get ya head & heart around these pages & make em work for ya !!

U can do the trad thing – & take one letter a day
thru' the month.

U can do the rad thing – & start at Z,
workin it back 2 A.

Or u can do the mad thing – & just hit it random, wotever, whenever, dip in & out; like switchin
channels on sky.

'Talk it' over ya fave ambient or dance trak.

Read it out LOUD at ya youth event 2 kick butt.

Wotever fries ya chips, hits the spot, quenches ya thirst 4 a chunk of God & girlstuff kickin it together.

U can keep goin back 2 it again & again, like an omnibus edition of ya fave soap. Rappin, readin or rememberin ya fave bits, the hardcore bits, the bits of the Bible that make ya wanna taste more!

Get God's voice loud & proud. Doesn't matter how u read it, but wot u do with wot u read. This book will mess up your life, it's not just all talk but all action. R u ready 4 it?

Feel the need, the need 2 read.

attitude

Bible bitz

Read Philippians 2:5
and Ephesians 4:20-24
Your attitude should be
the same as that of
Jesus Christ. (NIV)
To be made new in the
attitude of your minds.
(NIV)

Attitude – u can b rude, u can b crude, u can b in a mood.
Culture says 'b in2 urself, 4 urself, stuff the rest.'
It's all about u; get 2 the top; that's the zest.
Give as gud as u get, don't care who u hurt, b a selfish skirt!
Have a stinkin one 2wards lads, 2 ya teachers, ya parents,
ya carers, the church, ya leader, the dude who gets up ya nose,
ya past, now, the future – naff them all off, tell em where 2 go.
But the story don't end, it takes us round a bend,
turns u upside down; inside out; makes u shout.
Servin; sufferin; puttin urself last – that's the hardcore task.
We ain't like him – we sin – but we've got the power within,
2 change, 2 rearrange. Selflessness ain't strange
in our heads – our hearts – we gotta start,
2 do our part – get a tender heart –
2 b salt, 2 b light – we gotta b bright.
Stop stealin – tell the truth; attack anger – forgive;
feel his grace – outrageous & ace.
Glory in ya gob; ask God 2 make u sob, like Jesus hack the job –
the same as our hero, our love, our friend, our brother.
Live, & let others live.

chick chat

Dj Diva's spin of the day

So work it baby, eat humble
crumble, ready 2 rumble.
Go & find someone u need 2
apologise 2. Go & find someone
who is always doing it 4 u. Go
& put someone first, urself
last. Go & tell someone they r
the best, put it 2 the test.

9

b

bible

Bible bitz

<u>Read Hebrews 4:12</u>
His powerful Word is
sharp as a surgeon's
scalpel, cutting through
everything, whether
doubt or defense, laying
us open
to listen and obey.
(The Message)

Bounce ya booty through da Bible.
Boomin God & us, tells it how it is – no fuss –
the old & the nu scratchin it 2gether.
The dossier 2 colosse; the lads in Jesus posse;
the tribal desert crew & wot God thinks of u.
Sex, injustice, war & pain – y JC came 2 take the blame.
A nu head – a nu way; a nu heart – a nu day.
Getting down with wot God says; bringing on the rays
of son shine, 2 make ya feel fine.
Livin ya life; kickin strife; getting rife;
with life 2 the max – loadsa mad facts –
that will rock ya world & blow ya mind,
make ya a copy of the Jesus kind.
B a WOW Bird – a woman of the word –
get it in ya face, get in the book race –
it'll make u feel ace;
it'll shoot adrenalin in2 ur soul;
it'll sort ya head; it'll make ya whole.
It's called a hammer – a light, a sword – 2 chop off bits
that get ya in the pits, so go on & blitz!
Eat the word, girlstar, get it down ya neck,
chomp a bit everyday, it'll keep ya life in check.
Read it & weep, turn ya gud from bad.
Get the book & read it;
get the vid & watch it;
get the cd & listen 2 it;
whichever way it turns u on.
Make room 4 it – it makes room 4 u.

chick chat

Dj Diva's spin of the day

Listen 2 the old skool
track by the tribe called
'Eat the word' - it'll
rock ya pants!

choice

Bible bitz

Read Joshua 24:15

If you decide that it's a bad thing to
worship GOD, then choose a god you'd
rather serve - and do it today. Choose
one of the gods your ancestors worshipped
from the country beyond The River, or one
of the gods of the Amorites, on whose
land we are now living. As for me and my
family, we'll worship GOD.
(The Message)

Choices everywhere; wot 2 smell like; wot 2 wear?
Shud I use oxy? Shud I use soap?
Shud I drink booze? Shud I smoke dope?
Choose 2day who u live 4,
who's fryin yo chips?
Who's bangin ya door?
Who's influencing ya choices?
Wot's makin ya tick?
If someone is choosin 4 u – then giv em the flick.
Choose 2 lose or choose 2 win;
choose 2 get sorted or stay lovin sin.
U can ask God, but at the end of the day,
u decide wot game 2 play.
Ask him 2 push u in2 the right stuff
so u don't mess it up – cos life ain't no bluff!
Choose 2 back off or choose 2 fight,
choose 2 live wrong or choose 2 live right.
Wot's grabin ya passion? Wot's givin ya verve?
Givin up on ya dreams or getting some nerve?
Doin ya own thang or doin God's?
Pleasing ya Dad or pleasing ya bod?
Don't put it off, make the choice now.
Now is the time 2 put the P in Pow! (er)
God chose u, even when u didn't choose him,
keep hangin with JC – get his spirit deep in;
cos then the choices will kick in2 action,
a path that is cool with full satisfaction.
JC only did wot his Dad told him 2.
So can u.

chick chat

Dj Diva's spin of the day

Think about this –
'a gud choice isn't
always an easy voice.'
I believe in u girl,
make the right one.

dreamer

Bible bitz

Read Esther 4:14
Maybe you were made queen
for such a time as this.
(The Message)

Give us a D, 2 the R, 2 the E, 2 the A, 2 the M, 2 the E, 2 the R.
Check Esther, check Ruth, check loadsa truth.
Diva's of destiny with a big dream in mind.
Something cool, but something kind;
with God on ur side u r in 4 a wild ride.
Don't take life in ur stride, grab it before it hides.
A skatepark; a homeless hostel; a rape crisis centre;
a design workshop; a dance studio; a tv company;
a hip hop band; a football academy; ownin a magazine.
Wotever u're into, wotever rocks ur world;
wotever makes u angry; wotever u think is out of order;
wotever u wanna see change;
if u can't think then find somethin – anythin. Open ur eyes,
jump in2 action & dream 2 push others up & out from their pit,
so they can sit, where u r sittin – a daughter of the king
with a reason 2 sing.
Hearing negative voices about ur choices?
A negative person; a small mind; a gagging tradition;
a past failure; a fear of risk; a head jam;
'yeah right, u cud never do it – it'll never happen.
The big boys call it apathy; rationalism; cynicism;
play safe; kill wonder; kill dreams.
John, in the book of Revs in the Bible, says,
'come up higher,' – come on, man, see further,
see wot no one else sees, a higher purpose,
higher possibilities, a higher way of livin,
keep on keepin on, never never never give up
on urself or anyone else – God doesn't.
Walt Disney kept naggin the bank when he was
told 'NO' 2 borrow some cash 2 build mickey town –
he was told 'disney is so yesterday' – eat it now Mr Bankman!
Martin Luther King had a dream & rocked racism.
Gladys Aylward got told 'NO' from every Bible Association,
but went 2 China anyway & transformed kidz lives.

chick chat

Dj Diva's spin of the day

Get a local newspaper,
talk to people, see wot's
missin in ur community &
then START something!
Pray, listen, act!

evangelism

Bible bitz

Read Isaiah 61:1-4
and Matthew 28:18-20
He sent me to preach good news.
(The Message)
Go out and train everyone you meet,
far and near, in this way of life.
(The Message)

16

So the big fat 'E' word is in ya face - evangelism – eat it up baby.

Does it turn u on? does it turn u off?

The ideal – u're supposed 2 b up for it; mad about it; God, let me at it!

The real – pressure 2 blurb the ABC of redemption (wot?); pantzin it; scary as.

Maybe u can hack the rad?

Destiny Child style – lairy lyrics loud & proud,

'I'm not gonna compromise my Christianity.'

Maybe u can't hack the trad?

Singing cheesy songs in ya town centre;

'the end is near' being screamed from a soapbox;

gettin eaten by a rottweiler on door 2 door;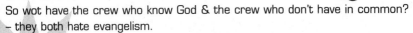

normal dudette in skool, transforms in2 damnation debbie,

on a mission from God – turn or burn.

So wot have the crew who know God & the crew who don't have in common?

– they both hate evangelism.

It's not worked;

still young people leave the church; hungry 4 something – but never gettin it.

'God is alive but he doesn't wanna get involved' graffitied on a wall,

God's naffed off & we're havin a ball. So wot's the score, does anyone know?

Our generation gets with God through a friend, not an event;

through love, not a leaflet; through belonging, not ear bashin;

through acceptance, not being judged.

Jesus says we gotta b gud news, not bad ass;

we gotta b a God flavour, not a bad odour;

we gotta bring colour 2 a grey world.

Check him out. Being gud news 2 a dodgy diva in the desert;

a rad & mad love; reachin out; speakin out; puttin God stuff about.

She woz a Samaritan (check John 4), she was a chick, in them days u didn't

talk 2 someone like that unless u were thick. Get Jesus – it made him tick.

The religious crew wud diss ya; they loved the trad; so he made em mad.

She needed water; he was where she was at; he gave her water; he gave her value;

he gave her dignity; he lifted her; her life changed; he was 'da man' – u r 'da girl'.

Dj Diva's spin of the day

So go & make someone's day. Have a laff; b a big heart;
smile at the bored out of her brains, chick cashier in top shop.
Pay 4 someone's sweets next 2 u in the queue; clean up the rubbish for ya
headteacher; make a brew 4 ya olds. Mow a garden; paint a garage;
lend ya bike out; ask 'are u ok?', 2 someone no one else talks 2 at skool.
Do somethin that culture ain't into - givin somethin 4 nothin; love
without condition. Salt ain't subtle, peanuts create thirst - b a peanut,
a thirst creator. Get a rad thing going on - u do give a stuff. It's
about givin before gabbin.
GO, GIVE, GAB & BLAB!

fear

Bible bitz

<u>Read 2 Timothy 1:7
and Proverbs 14:27</u>
For God did not give us
a spirit of timidity,
but a spirit of power,
of love and of
self-discipline.
(NIV)

2 kindsa fear r near, comin at ya from da rear.
1 is God's kind, with love, power & a sound mind.
'Fear of the Lord' means respek 2 him – phat awe –
being God-smacked by him; it's him u want more.
Fear is the start of wisdom – biggin up the king –
he's the grandmaster mixer, the maker of everythin.
Take ya chunky shoes off – this is holy ground –
with God u can do anything, so get ur head around
the enemies plans 2 take u out,
but wiv God u got no worries, no doubts.
Strutt in ya armour, make him know wot u're about.
God is watchin ya back; keeping ya from attack;
but don't giv the enemy slack 2 whack.
Cos his fear is dark – the put-u-down kind –
it grabs ya heart & jams ya mind.
It lies with a capital L. It says u won't live 2 tell
the story of God's glory
in u & on u, givin u hope, makin u nu.
Tell the enemy 2 chew, tell him 2 stew;
cos when ya jump he'll catch ya;
if u fall he's there;
he gives ya 'no buts' 2 leave fear behind;
he gives ya the guts 2 DARE.
So face ya fears – don't drag on 4 years.
Naff off the stuff that holds u down;
get a phat smile – lose the frown.
Don't let ya fears stand in the way of ya dreams;
when God says 'u can', that's wot he means.
So believe it, grab it, keep it real.
U got one hit, that's the deal.
'My perfect love gets rid of fear.' (says God)
'B gutsy girl, cos I am near.'

chick chat

Dj Diva's spin of the day

Get a 'No Fear'
snowboarding poster on ya wall
that says 'face ya fears
live ya dreams'
& think about it!

gossip

Read Proverbs 21:23
Watch your words
and hold your tongue;
you'll save yourself
a lot of grief.
(The Message)

Gossip is bad, makes God mad;
it stirs stuff up, makes God sad.
Choose life or death in ya tongue –
it's up 2 u – but its wrong 2 pong
of 'hav u heard' or 'listen 2 this' –
a 2-faced girl with a 2-faced kiss.
Don't say 'we need 2 pray 4 her & that's y I'm telling u'.
It's dodgy ground 2 blag God's name – if u do, u is a fool.
It can b sweet, It can b sour;
makin someone cower, then praisin the next hour.
Check the motive in ya heart before u 2 start 2 goss;
2 open ya lips, wiv attitude on ya hips.
Remember who's ya boss;
think before u gob, who r u gonna rob
or who ya gonna hurt, by dishin up some dirt?
Say it 2 someone's face, if u have a prob.
Doin wot the word says, that's wot does the job.
B loyal – believe the best – that's the gutsy test;
2 find out 4 yurself & put bad stuff 2 rest.
Gud girl goss, no gloss, no floss.
Hav a mouth like Jesus, check the cross.
Ain't got nothing gud 2 say? say nothing at all,
then u'll stand tall; u'll have a ball; u won't fall.
So sista, don't spit, don't have a fit, about someone
who gets up ya nose – don't giv em verbal blows.
Make the choice 2 quieten ya voice;
zip it shut; don't get in a rut.
Seal the deal & keep it real.

Dj Diva's spin of the day

Girlfriend!
If u ain't got nothing gud 2 say,
then say nothing at all – get me?

holy

Bible bitz

<u>Read 1 Peter 1:13-16</u>
God said, 'I am holy; you be holy.
(The Message)

Holy ground; a holy sound;
livin in the light;
getting rid of bad stuff
that tangles up ya life;
it might b a book; it might b a lad;
it might b a vid that gets ya dead mad.
So ur thinking 'where is God?
I can't feel him anymore.'
But he ain't moved, girlfriend,
u gotta know the score.
It hurts God when we diss him,
when we do the compromise,
come on girl, get it sorted,
so the light in u can rise.
Holiness is happiness – u ain't no boring freak.
He is holy; he is jealous; he wants u girl 2 seek
his face in the place;
pressin on in the race.
Holy livin; godly givin;
doin it Jehovah style.
Constant trippin on the things of the king,
not just doin it 4 a while.
Does God like u hot or does God like u cold?
Does God like u inbetween
or get in2 it when ya old?
No way, Hosea, all the h's r in the house –
holy, hot & happy –
so shake it all about.

chick chat

Dj Diva's spin of the day

Take an honest look at urself
& decide wot u need
2 sort out in ya life.
Then DO IT!

image

Bible bitz

<u>Read Genesis 1:27</u>
Let us make human beings
in our image,
make them reflecting our nature.
(The Message)

So u got a pash for fash(ion);
2 flash ur cash; buy something rash –
Gucci, versace, red or dead,
long hair, curly, or a messy bed head.
8.9 billion pounds, the beauty industry is doin the rounds
2 make ya unhappy with who u r;
2 do ur head in with 'if u buy this u'll go far.'
Dress 2 impress, or dress 2 kill;
tryin 2 keep 'in' can get ya ill.
Wantin 2 b thinner, prettier, fitter –
comparing can make u bitter.
Stressin over the size of ur butt, can get u in a rut;
J Lo keeps her cool when people wanna fool,
with how her butt shud look, by the book.
'NO' is wot she shouts, no regrets, no doubts!
So celebrate ur boobs & celebrate ur thighs.
Make the choice 2 b individual, stop comparin, kick the lies,
that u have 2 b the same as models in the mags,
who ain't real anyway – a computer retouch in the bag.
Kick the manipulation, don't b sucked in2 a nation
that puts value on the outside, don't get taken 4 a ride.
Beauty is only skin deep, not something u can keep.
Real beauty is about the inside, bout ur pash 4 life;
bout playin on God's side, ur thumbprint gives u pride.
No one can live ur life like u,
so start 2 accept urself – b new.
In finding out who u are,
without the gear or Nokia.
A daughter of the king – u ain't no ming;
U r unique – u ain't no freak;
God sings over u – u ain't no mistake;
U r a real life princess – u ain't no fake.
So girls, everyday, look at wot God says.
Get his voice loud & proud – not the crowds –
eat the word – b a 'God sings over me' bird.
Make the mirror ur friend
that'll drive the enemy round the bend.

chick chat

Dj Diva's spin of the day

Check out & write out all the verses about how God sees u, on a phat bit
of paper. Start with Jeremiah 1:5; Matthew 10:29-31 and Romans 8:38, then
find some more. Stick them up in ya bedroom, bathroom, filofax - wherever.
Then read it out loud everyday 2 yurself -
it'll rock ya world!

jesus

Bible bitz

<u>Read Hebrews 12:2</u>
Keep your eyes on Jesus,
who both began and
finished this race we're in.
Study the way he did it.
(The Message)

Jesus, G-sus – he's the man –
if he can't do it, no one can.
He's got the power & he's got the guts
2 free u, sort u, get u out of ruts.
He ain't white, and he shines bright,
cos he's the light, that'll make u right.
He's the door – the lover of the poor;
he's the bread of life – feeds ya heart & head;
he's the son of God – he didn't stay dead.
2 teach wot real life is about;
2 give a stuff about the minger;
2 give time 2 talk 2 the tart;
2 not mess with religion stuff.
But b rad & set apart,
2 b like him, 2 love & 2 forgive,
2 push the limits in the way u live.
JC kicked it, rocked it, didn't just sit.
Did wot his dad said in one hit.
He's there for u, he understands;
he's sorted ur future, he's got mad plans.
Loneliness; rejection; love & pain –
he's been there girl, he's felt the same.
Chuck off the past; dump the dross;
get down with JC – the boss of the cross.
So run 2 him, with him, 4 him.
Get a rage in ur belly, don't give a nelly
wot people think, when they make a stink
bout u doin it JC style 4 more than a while.

chick chat

Dj Diva's spin of the day

Get 2 know him –
not just know about him.
Treat him like u treat ur bezzie mate –
wiv respek on top.

kiss

Bible bitz

<u>Read Proverbs 24:26</u>
An honest answer
is like a kiss on the lips.
(NIV)

Kiss my hand, kiss my face,
kiss my lips, leave a trace.
Barbie & Ken, sittin in a tree k. i. s. s. i. n. g;
but where does that leave me?
Never been kissed, is my fame;
dunno how 2 play the game.
Pressure 2 have ur first can make u thirst;
can make u gag; cos u wanna brag.

chick chat

How do u know how 2 hold ur head,
or open or close ur mouth instead.
The mags put u under pressure –
u gotta kiss like this or that,
if u wanna get a lad,
if u wanna b gud not bad –
kick the pressure, just b u.
If it's time 2 get a kiss,
& u r feelin like a freak,
chill out & let him lead.
Take it slow, no need 4 speed,
she who dares wins; kissin ain't no sin.
But guard ur heart – u r set apart;
ur lips r the lords – not the hordes.
b picky – make it tricky;
then u know it's 4 real – it's ace!
A God kiss is a boom where 2 hearts pound,
2 beats 2 the tune, the breath is the sound.
2 lives filled with passion 4 life & God –
respectin each other, respectin ur bods.
A kiss is like an honest answer –
in ya face & nice.
A kiss betrayed Jesus, a kiss gave him up,
a kiss made Jesus drink
of a suffering cup.
So b aware of what a kiss can do,
be a girl with a head that's clued!

Dj Diva's spin of the day

My first kiss wasn't till I was 18 –
so chill with the still –
right things happen at the right time –
God ain't ever early or late!
So trust in God's timing
and b accountable 2 ur mates.

love

Bible bitz

Read 1 Corinthians 13
Love never gives up.
(The Message)

Love ain't gooey; love ain't fluffy;
love ain't sex; love ain't wussy;
love ain't Hollywood; love ain't elvis;
love ain't a quick snog, or jivin ya pelvis.
Love is doin something that is all talk, all action;
love is about servin, top satisfaction;
love is a giver – God is love,
bangin down from heaven,
in ur face its shoved.
U can't diss it, run away from it,
get ur head around it or take a bit.
Cos it's the love massive,
u can't b passive.
U don't deserve it or earn it by bein gud.
It's chucked at u freely – hung on bits of wood.

chick chat

The L 2 the E is packed with GRACE –
love never ending is in the place.
Nothing can separate u from its pace,
not even when u naff off from runnin the race.
It's always there 2 get u in2 a dare,
2 push the limits – go the extra mile;
love the person up ur nose –
put a lid on the fake smile;
chase true love – & follow hard.
Love is havin a grateful heart,
so start 2 see mates as God sees them –
see the inside, see the gem.
Don't b ripped off,
by a love that is cheap
& easy 2 find cos its not gonna keep.
It goes off like a sell-by date!
Compared 2 God's love –
no competition – it don't rate!

Dj Diva's spin of the day

B an all talk, all action girl –
if u can't do it then don't say
it till u can.
Go out & do something for someone
4 no reason & see em smile.

mista

Bible bitz

<u>Read Genesis 2:7</u>
The Man came alive - a living soul.
(The Message)

chick chat

Sista, u want a mista?
Ur best mate, u miss her,
cos she's got a lad – who ain't half bad –
makes u glad – but makes u sad –
cos u want some lovin
n ur ears – sweet nothings.
Girl! single 2 mingle is a top place 2 b!
Make the most of ur time, while u r kickin it free.
Don't play a desperate diva or wait around
for a lad 2 come ur way – b a girl who is sound.
The best is worth the wait – so don't take the bait
of thinkin u have 2 have one NOW –
2 the posse of 'couples' u have 2 bow.
When God decides 2 bring in MR RITE
it'll b alright on the night – no frights.
for u that struggle – seein is believin –
when there ain't no LOG's (lads of God) around its deceivin,
that God can bring someone out of the wood;
his timin is perfect – it'll happen like it shud.
Boyfriend, boyf, u gotta choice,
listen 2 ur inner voice.
Whose shud ya choose?
Is he on the booze?
Is he in2 stuff thats gonna make it ruff?
Bloke, lad, geezer, dude,
make sure he's a lad of God;
make sure he ain't rude.
U can go with a lad who ain't in2 God,
but it'll b tuff 2 stay pure – b tuff on ya bod.
Don't go 4 wot car he drives or if he can cook,
don't go 4 image, don't go 4 looks.
Go 4 his passion 4 God and the lost,
Mr luvva will respek u wotever it costs.
If he treats u like a princess,
then u won't b in a mess –
honour, respek –
not bullied or decked.

Dj Diva's spin of the day

Battle with the urge 2 merge by hangin
with loadsa mates - get a life full of
God stuff - don't settle 4 anything less
than the best - its worth the wait!
I found my Mr Rite when I was 31!

notion

Bible bitz

Read Acts 2:14-17
'In the last days,' God says,
'I will pour out my Spirit
on every kind of people...'
(NIV)

Get a notion (an idea),
cause a commotion;
get with God's potion
with an IDEA that'll shake this nation.
Somethin nu; somethin fresh;
b a girl of innovation –
4 ur skool; 4 the fools
who say there is no God.
Slap on some lotion,
of the son kind,
that shook the temple,
gave sight 2 the blind –
open ur mouth, God will fill it;
zoom round ya classroom,
God will hit it.
Run out of ideas; held back by ur fears;
get ur butt in2 gear – let God steer.
Make a noise, keep ya poise,
cos u only get one go
at life – so do it rite.
Don't miss a chance
2 strutt ur funky stuff,
2 kick off somethin in ur skool
that yells out 'God is e nuff.'
Givin, servin, lovin, livin.
Don't miss out on God's thang,
cos u got it goin on girl.
Bang the beats and start 2 sing;
God's call 4 u 2 make it tall;
ideas from his head just fall.
2 shake & break & take –
b the icin on God's cake.
No stoppin at the station –
notion 4 a nation.

Dj Diva's spin of the day

Have a brainstormin sesh –
write down all ur ideas & do
something original!

chick chat

overcome

Bible bitz

<u>Read Revelation 12:10-12</u>
They defeated him through the blood of the Lamb
and the bold word of their witness.
(The Message)

Depression – havin a bad session.
Feelin naff, feelin crap, feelin in a trap.
Taken out; pulled down; the enemy is sittin on ya head;
he's givin u a frown; wishin u were dead.
BUT God's got something 2 say, comin on strong,
it'll hit u in ya heart, it'll kick out all the wrong
thoughts that say 'this is the end.'
'there ain't no way out or something round the bend.'
If God says it, then it's gotta b gud,
so get with the truth – the hope in the hood.
'U r more than a conqueror' with a capital C
livin 2 win, knockin on 10 outta 10.
U r a winner in Christ; who made the sacrifice;
who kicked butt on the cross – no fuss, no gloss –
so u can lift ur chin up, cos it's in his strength u fight.
Get ya armour on, cos the JC price was right.
Get overcomin – start the runnin.
Bouncin high – reach 4 the sky.
Phat faith in ur heart – u got the part
of winner, of chooser, of freegirl, not loser.
No matter wot ur sitch, when ur in a ditch,
Jesus overcame – he got the same.
Dark attacks, 2 knock u back
from the enemy, tryin 2 keep u down.
But RISE up – u can take on the town –
cos everyplace u go, God is with the flow;
ur confidence in him – doubt hits the bin.
Believe him when he says (u r more...)
cos these r the joy dayz.

chick chat

p

pure

Bible bitz

Read Psalm 24:4
He who has clean hands
and a pure heart,
who does not lift up his soul
to an idol or
swear by what is false.
(NIV)

Pure, lets get raw.
It's tuff – it's hardcore.
In a world that is tainted
u gotta b MISS PURE.
Stay cool with God's word – which is true,
wedded before bedded – b one of the few.
Got the urge 2 merge? Hold on don't splurge,
the narrow road is hard but cool –
so don't fool with the cool,
cos the cool don't fool.
Don't mess – God knows wot's best.
Put it 2 the test:
respect urself; respect ur bod;
if u get under pressure – shout 2 God –
cos there ain't no temptation that u can't handle –
let ur Jesus stylee sparkle.
'Get behind me, dude. This ain't ur ride';
'I got God in me – go take a stride';
'Wot part of NO don't u understand?'
tell it 2 him straight – in his face & canned.
Born again virgin; born again head;
born again heart; born again cred.
A pure princess is wot u r,
if u've said 'Soz God' u r goin far.
God is the restorer of ur soul –
sortin ur mind, will & emotions is his goal.
So u can live in the core of his love,
gettin cleaned up, forgiven, made nu by his blood.
So girl get ya face up, bounce around ya room,
kick some kingdom in ur head, then u'll rise & shine & bloom.

chick chat

Dj Diva's spin of the day

Get in the shower with ya fave shower gel
& pray off the stuff u know is
messin up ya life while u is soakin
in the suds! It feels the bomb!

quest

Bible bitz

Read Matthew 28:18-20
All authority in heaven and on earth
has been given to me.
Therefore go and make
disciples of all nations.
(NIV)

Here comes a test
2 see how much zest
u got, in the pot,
2 chill and rot, or get off ya bot.
Get on a journey that's hot,
with passion, guts and determination
2 rock ur nation,
with the gospel that is gud news –
rocked the temple, rocks the pews.
God can do more than u ask or imagine –
so get on up like a faith machine.
Get mean; get tight; stay up all night,
24/7 prayin ya pants off;
diggin ur generation, out of the trough.
Wot r u in2? Wot r u about?
Don't just play about like a lazy trout.
Flippin shout at injustice;
get angry at pain;
take the less out of homeless;
get in on the game.
U'll never b the same
cos Jesus lives in u –
think about it, let it stew.
He said, u can do MORE than he did:
he healed; he spat on eyes, they saw;
he raised the dead; he ran ahead,
with God's plans in his hands,
2 sacrifice – pay a price.
Layin down his life was in no way nice.
But paid off – ripped the cloth.
A big quest, with a big Q.
So it's comin on strong –
wot r u gonna do?

chick chat

Dj Diva's spin of the day

Check out wot is goin on
for young people in ur area – & where
there is a gap – start something!

41

rad

Bible bitz

<u>Read John 2:12-25</u>
Jesus put together a whip
out of strips of leather
and chased them out of the Temple.
(The Message)

Is rad gud or is rad bad?
Does God like it? Does it rock the trad?
Is it being controversial just cos it's cool?
Is it wisdom or is it a fool?
Rad can make u glad – gettin mad
at a hurtin world – dyin and in pain –
radical action brings the healin rain.
Livin on the edge, not goin with the flow,
u can play safe or u can play 2 'GO'.
In2 the world; gettin involved,
with the unlovable; lives unresolved.
A rad love; a rad attitude religious find rude;
hangin with the smelly dude; hangin with the crude.
Bein in the world, not of. Still goin 2 the party;
gettin down with the trends, but not lookin tarty;
not gettin drunk as a skunk or snoggin a slamin hunk;
but doin a bunk from the religious bubble,
that keeps u outta trouble (they say), but outta touch,
with real lives that need 2 get some Jesus.
Abused; neglected; rejected; suspected; sussed.
The frontline; gives shudders down ya spine;
sin in ya face; tackle it – it's ace!
'The sick need a doctor,' was somethin JC said.
So open ur eyes; listen 2 the cries; don't just stay in bed.
When someone hurts u, turn ur cheek;
u gotta journey 2 forgive, u gotta play meek.
That takes guts, no BUTS, no ifs, no shuds.
A radical life, flows from radical blood.

chick chat

Dj Diva's spin of the day

Go 2 a party –
don't get drunk –
but b the best laff there!
& when ya mates ask wot u're on –
tell em JC.

43

secure

Bible bitz

Read Deuteronomy 33:12
Let the beloved of the LORD
rest secure in him.

Bein secure ain't no bore.
It roots ya down, makes ya sound
in ya mind & heart, so u don't start
2 stress or strop or worry at the top,
that ur world will crumble if there's a rumble
of getting dumped or failing exams –
God knows girl, he understands.
Cos with God u're safe, he's holding u tight;
he makes it alright; don't b scared at nite.
When he says jump, u say how high.
He says he'll give u eagles wings 2 fly
above situations, above the tuff stuff of life;
or get ya head around a changing world,
that gives u hassle, makes u cry.
His shoulders r like boulders –
u can trust him every time.
He's got his groove on – takes everything in his stride.
'Chuck ya cares at me – cos I care for u.' Jesus says.
He doesn't want u 2 worry anyway or anyday.
He's ur security – ur identity;
he's ya rock when u r shaky;
he's ya shelter when u're thinking
'my life is feelin quaky.'
U get secure – there is a cure –
by restin in him –
no stressing, no din.
So ask him, let him in
2 the areas where u don't feel it.
Where u're in an insecure pit
when u react 2 how u look,
or wot someone says;
that puts ya in a trap – spending ur dayz,
feelin jealous.
Giv it up girl – see urself in God's eyes.
B thankful, 4 wot God has done 4 u –
made u, given u,
press on & get a surprise!

chick chat

Dj Diva's spin of the day

The only way 2 get secure, girl, is 2 know who u r in God
& accept ur bod - so get them daughter of the king verses in u & ur
confidence will pump up the volume of feelin secure.
Try out: Psalm 61:2,3; Psalm 46:1,2 & John 10:27-29

truth

Bible bitz

<u>Read John 8:31,32</u>
Then you will know the truth,
and the truth will set you free.
(NIV)

Truth with a capital T,
that's wot sets u free.
Jesus with a phat 'J',
follow him – he's the way.
2 gettin ur head & heart sorted;
so a messed up life gets aborted;
cos he gives ya a nu one, 2 brew, 2 chew
on the things that r true.
The truth about why u r here,
the truth about God is near.
Even when u mess up & feel naff,
when u feel u ain't nothin more than riff-raff.
C the devil is the father of lies,
with his sneaky demon spies,
tryin 2 get u not 2 believe,
tryin 2 get u 2 b deceived.
In2 thinkin naff thoughts about urself & God,
so u never get in2 serious time in ur POD (place of discipleship).
Believe Jesus instead, see the RED,
so ur life is in the light, then u can fight,
the enemy's foxy schemes,
2 take away ya son beams –
darken down ya gleams.
The truth is always wot it seems,
wot u see is wot u get,
even if u don't see it yet.
Get some TROOF, YOOF,
it'll blow off ya ROOF!

Dj Diva's spin of the day

GET IN2 YA BIBLE –
that's the place u'll get TRUTH –
expect 2 know who u r
& wot u're about – GET A LIFE!

Psalm 139

For the director of music.
Of David. A psalm.

O LORD, you have searched me
and you know me.

You know when I sit and when I rise;
you perceive my thoughts from afar.

You discern my going out and my lying down;
you are familiar with all my ways.

Before a word is on my tongue
you know it completely, O LORD.

You hem me in – behind and before;
you have laid your hand upon me.

Such knowledge is too wonderful for me,
too lofty for me to attain.

Where can I go from your Spirit?
Where can I flee from your presence?

If I go up to the heavens, you are there;
if I make my bed in the depths, you are there.

If I rise on the wings of the dawn,
if I settle on the far side of the sea,

even there your hand will guide me,
your right hand will hold me fast.

If I say, "Surely the darkness will hide me
and the light become night around me,"

even the darkness will not be dark to you;
the night will shine like the day,
for darkness is as light to you.

For you created my inmost being;
you knit me together in my mother's womb.

I praise you because I am fearfully and wonderfully made;
your works are wonderful,
I know that full well.

My frame was not hidden from you
when I was made in the secret place.
When I was woven together in the depths of the earth,

your eyes saw my unformed body.
All the days ordained for me
were written in your book
before one of them came to be.

How precious to me are your thoughts, O God!
How vast is the sum of them!

Were I to count them,
they would outnumber the grains of sand.
When I awake,
I am still with you.

If only you would slay the wicked, O God!
Away from me, you bloodthirsty men!

They speak of you with evil intent;
your adversaries misuse your name.

Do I not hate those who hate you, O LORD,
and abhor those who rise up against you?

I have nothing but hatred for them;
I count them my enemies.

Search me, O God, and know my heart;
test me and know my anxious thoughts.

See if there is any offensive way in me,
and lead me in the way everlasting. (NIV)

u

Bible bitz

Read Psalm 139
(previous page)
You have searched me
and you know me.
(NIV)

U, you, one in a few (million!),
don't matter wot people say about u.
U r the D in daughter, the P in princess –
get ur head around this, or b in a mess.
Wot matters is wot God says – check out the nu,
ctuff off the past, live 4 today,
that's the kickin thang to do.
U r the U in unique – no G in geek!
God knew u, before u were born –
in ya mums belly,
bouncing round in jelly.
He saw u & he loved u,
every moment of ur dayz.
He knew he had mad plans for u,
in ur work, ur love, ur play.
U r the apple of his eye,
u make his heart beat fast,
cos u r unique,
he only made one cast.
If the creator chose to bake,
u'd b the cherry on his cake.
With his digital zoom lens,
it's ur picture he wud take.
U r honoured & u're precious,
u're special in his eyes.
He always sees the best in u –
he's proper on ur side.
He's down with the number of hairs on ya head,
he's cool knowin when u get in & out of bed.
Cos no one else has ur thumbprint,
no one else has got ur face,
no one else got wot u got –
God thinks u rock, u're ace!

chick chat

Dj Diva's spin of the day

I've said it before, but I'll bang on
about it again until u get it!
Check out the verses in the Bible that
tell u who u r & how God feels about u –
that's the truth, that's true freedom!
ARE U DOIN IT YET OR WOT?
Check Zephaniah 3:17 to start.

vocation

Bible bitz

Read Matthew 6:25
Is not life more important
than food, and the body
more important than clothes?
(NIV)

Wot's ya vocation
means wot's ya job.
Wot's ya future like –
a career head or blob?
People talk about gettin God's will;
well it ain't no pill
that is hard 2 swallow, that will make u sick –
it'll make u tick –
cos God's given u passion,
he's given u zest,
he knows wot u like,
put it 2 the test.
Inspired, fired, wired, not tired –
think in sync with God,
where does he want ya smile, ya bod –
stop stressin, trust – that's a must.
God's got it sorted, divine plans imported –
UK, Africa, New York,
there ain't no lines, no chalk –
u r told 2 Go, full stop –
waiting 4 a divine map is a cop

chick chat

out, that's not wot u're about.
Go wiv God is always right,
choose 2 cruise, sit tight –
uni, 6th form, 2 do 4 wot I was born,
keep it simple, keep it real.
Wot is it that givs ya 'yeah baby' appeal?
Go 4 that, the world ain't flat!
Don't worry if it turns out wrong,
cos God will always bring u back,
turn ya around,
put u on the right track,
2 the thing u shud b doin –
on the chomp u shud b chewin.
There's not only one plan, man,
so get in the car or get in the van.

Dj Diva's spin of the day

Find out info on everything & anything.
Lay it out on the table & choose wot
fries ya chips - makes u tick!

w

wonder

(Bible bitz)

Read Isaiah 29:14
I will astound these people
with wonder upon wonder.
(NIV)

The nu Wonder Bra makes boobs go far,
Wonder woman can pick up a car!
Wonderstuff gobsmacks you,
makes u go 'ah'.
It's about gettin rid of the block in ur head,
that makes u indifferent,
makes ur heart dead.
2 the world around u – the power of God;
2 realisin ur value –
bein thankful 4 wot u got;
seein things fresh – God makin nu;
the wonder of life – the wonder of u.
big eyed wonder – realisin life ain't no blunder –
the ordinary, the norm,
gets alive, gets re-born.
Wonder is about wide-eyed expectation,
the childlike faith movin ur nation.
Where small things exite,
like stars in the nite,
knowin God loves u big,
u got treasures, u dig?
Can't get ur head around it –
it blows u away;
it makes u sit up, make a play 4 today,
cos u don't own 2morra,
it might not come ur way.
When u lose wonder, u lose ur soul –
nothin gets u going, ur heads in a hole.
Don't appreciate, don't rate anythin;
u don't thank, u ain't grateful or love livin.
But listen girl, there's more, that's the score
2 havin been there, done that, got the t-shirt –
so kick some familiar dirt,
put on a wonderskirt!

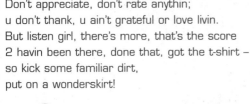

Dj Diva's spin of the day

Look at ya life – b grateful
for where u've come from
& wot u've got –
the small things open ur eyes.

xtreme

[Bible bitz]

<u>Read John 10:10</u>
A thief is only there to
steal and kill and destroy.
(NIV)

Xtreme can make u angry,
issues that get u off ur butt.
Xtreme can make u green,
stoppin the trees being cut.
Xtreme pushes the levels, gives room
2 dare without a care or a snare,
2 have no limits.
Young souls rebel, like pebbles,
everyone different – causing a dent
on the beach. It seems out of reach
but they show
us how 2 grow – kickin miss average
in2 touch.
Givin 100% is never 2 much.
Xtreme rain – massive ark;
xtreme light – shone in the dark;
Jesus – the xtreme bright spark.
John the Baptist – an xtreme voice in the desert,
livin a life that wasn't that pleasant,
eatin locusts, wearing skins –
a radical dude bringin Jesus in.
Xtreme measures 2 save the world –
gave his only son, his plan unfurled.
B xited about being united,
2 the maker, the creator,
the perpetrator
of the XTREME scene –
don't forget 2 lean (over the edge)!

chick chat

Dj Diva's spin of the day

Take up an xtreme sport –
there ain't no natural buzz like it!
– or find a green issue u can support.

y?

Bible bitz

Read Job 11:7
Can you fathom
the mysteries of God?
(NIV)

Y? Why?
t's ok 2 b angry, it's ok 2 cry,
and not understand wot's goin on.
So u feel like God has packed up & gone
2 planet zog, or on the bog?
Or miles way 'up there' – don't even care?
It's better 2 b honest & real with him,
than gettin all bitter & let attitude move in.
Cos a hard heart won't get u nowhere,
make u lose & not choose ur dad,
who knows the bad
u r on about.

chick chat

U r allowed 2 shout u know –
u don't have 2 pretend.
I bet blaggin drives God round the bend,
cos he knows wot u're thinking &
y u feel stinking with questions u can't answer right now.
Check Dave in the Bible, he wrote the psalms.
He shouted at God, he said he had quarms
about stuff that was goin down in his life,
like when he murdered a geezer
cos he'd slept with his wife.
But then he looks up –
dances naked, shows his butt.
Undignified he realises that its only God who pleases.
Come on Dave – get with the rave.
'Y r u down my soul' he says 2 himself –
'yet I will praise him no matter wot,
even if I lose my face & wealth.'
God knows the score – bein in the desert is a bore.
But its where he grabs ya attention,
where u start 2 giv him a mention.
Cos maybe when u're angry, u push him out ur face,
u stop gaggin 2 hang wiv him & keeping up the pace.
So he ain't moved – he's still in ur groove –
don't matter wot u feel, cos that's the deal.
Believe it or not – that's up 2 u –
u can choose life or u can choose poo!

Dj Diva's spin of the day

Hav a chat with God & b honest about how u feel
& why u r angry – that's ok, that's the real
deal – he knows anyway – u r his daughter.

Z

zzzzz

Bible bitz

<u>Read Ephesians 5:14</u>
Wake up from your sleep,
Climb out of your coffins.
(The Message)

Sleep can b deep, can keep u dozin.
While u r layin low, the world out there is posin.
The voices of 'y am I here?' 'God is borin'
the church is out – I can hear the snoring!'
Wake up o sleeper & God will shine on u
2 bring salvation 2 the masses –
who need a life that's nu.
Sleep in ya eyes, get up & RISE!
Strike a God pose, Jesus arose,
came alive, he didn't take a dive.
U can survive or thrive or live in a hive,
bein a Christian fat cat,
getting fed up with this or that.
Cd's, posters, tapes & books,
the t-shirts getting thin.
Chillin wiv ur God stuff while ur mates
don't get a look in
the zeds keep u content.
Cos u're happy where u r,
don't wanna rock the boat 2 much,
don't wanna go 2 far.
Cos a Jesus Freak is freaky,
& the God squad sounds not cool.
U'd rather sleep & eat in fluffyland,
let them sit there till they drool – at skool,
with no fuel 4 life,
then u wonder y?
U wonder y they die.
Maybe its time 2 set ur alarm.
Ditch the duvet, get up & try.

chick chat

Jackie Pullinger had no cash 2 flash, but she had pash, for God.
He turned it in 2 a pash 2 see the drug addicts finding a nu buzz
in Jesus.
B a diva who dreams, do it large, go 4 the blue sky.
Hav guts, no buts, don't wishful think, chase ya dream,
naff off 'wotever', stuff 'yeah right'.
Is culture's voice bigger in u than God's?
Don't let fears stand in the way of ur dreams.
If u have a constipated imagination – u need a God laxative!
A unique mix of faith, passion & real deal spirit. With man things r
impossible but with God everything is possible – with God u CAN!
Wot part of 'U can' don't u understand?
Dream, then deliver.

So get pash & get rash; get holy anger; get a hunger panger;
write it down.
Imagine it; breath it; live it; work ur butt off. Pray cos it all depends
on God & work like it all depends on u!
Now is the time.
Talk about it; go on about it; till someone listens.
It's not about where u're from – it's about where u're standin.
It's not about where u hav been – it's about where u're goin.
The difference between the past & the future is,
u can change the future – GO GIRL.

Rad & mad brings out the 'Y?' in ur mates. 'Y does she talk 2 me
when no one else does?' 'Y did she bother when no one else in my life
bothers?' 'Y doesn't she diss me?' So they're askin; they're listenin;
with fat ears; with big wonder; they wanna know y u do wot u do. U've
done the givin, so now u do the gabbin. Ya open ya mouth; God fills it;
like he says in Psalm 81:10. U say it clear, u say it simple, u keep it
real – it's Jesus – he's done stuff 4 me, so I'm doing it 4 u – large!

Girl International

Girl International is a national organisation based in the centre of the universe – the Norf-West! (Stoke-on-Trent). It is headed up by Dawnie Reynolds-Deaville (Girl International) and assisted by Emma Owen (The Tribe). Girl International was birthed from Soulsista – an initiative that Dawnie & Emma ran, supported by The Message & Soul Survivor, which saw 2000 girls down souf checking out God. Now after a few years of change in direction, location, babies, weddings & girliestuff, a nu vision has emerged into the nu stylee Girl International – c,mon!

    Girl International is about realisin ya value, reaching ya potential & rockin ya world – go girl!!

    Its in ya face style & content aims to hit the hardcore bitz of ya life & give ya wot ya need to be a rockin Girl of God in this generation.

    Girl International is about God, gloss & gud girl goss! They run:

    Local events – an innovative mix of chat, interviews, guests, wild worship, competitions, social action & more, held in Stoke-on-Trent every 6 weeks – come take a sneaky peek!

    The Big Gig – a national event 4 girls 13+ doin it live & large with top speakers, guests, bands, sassy seminars, workshops, fashion, resources & more!

    Girls on tour – if you want a speaker, a dj, a singer, a dancer at an event, then u can book the girls 2 come & see u.

    Hey Girl CD – 'Hey Girl' is the title track on this kickin issue based CD banged out by The Tribe & produced by Alliance Music. It rocks, with some top tunes by girls of God like Superchick, T-Girl & others, check out ya local christian bookstore.

    Girl clothing – funk it, with fairly traded fashion with a range of phat T-shirts, hoodies & accessories.

for more info contact

Dawnie Reynolds-Deaville
dj1@girlinternational.com
www.girlinternational.com

U can be transformed
Meet God thru the Bible
B changed
D-TOX your community
Change others
D-TOX the world
Change the world

www.d-tox.org.uk